WHEN THE COPS COME KNOCKIN'

An Illustrated Guide to Criminal Law

School and Organization Edition Activity Book

Written by Travis & Trinity Townsend

Torinity Publishing Company
3645 Marketplace Blvd.
Suite 130-333
East Point, GA 30344
Tel: 1-800-552-0762

www.copscomeknockin.com

©2010

A book designed to teach young people (and anyone else) about criminal law, the criminal justice system, and their legal rights

TORINITY

First published 2010 by Torinity, LLC. Printed in the United States of America.

ISBN: 978-0-9835224-1-6

DISCLAIMER

Warning: the explanations provided throughout *When The Cops Come Knockin'* are not intended to be precise recitations of the law, but instead are loose, worst-case–scenario translations of the law aimed at giving the reader a surface understanding of the law. The definitions of specified laws in this book are loosely based on the model penal code and common law and may not be in effect in the jurisdiction and city where you live. By writing this book, we are not providing legal advice and do not attempt to provide legal advice. Readers assume the risk of acting upon the information found in *When The Cops Come Knockin'*. We recommend you contact an attorney with respect to any and all of the subject matter inside this book for clarification, and if you find yourself in legal trouble, hire an attorney immediately or, if you can't afford one, ask to have the court appoint an attorney to you immediately!

Table of Contents

PART I

CRIMES AND CRIMINAL OFFENSES

NAME _____ DATE _____

PART I: CRIMES AND CRIMINAL OFFENSES

PRE-TEST

Fill in the Blank

Directions

Please fill in the blanks with the correct answer.

1. A _Crqmal_ is the classification given a person after committing a crime.

2. _Laws_ are government rules to keep order and protect people.

3. _Not Knowing_ is no excuse for breaking the law.

4. _Striing_ is the taking of somebody else's property with the intent to keep it.

5. _____ _____ occurs when you ignore clues and facts that would alert you that you are doing, or are about to do, something unlawful.

6. A crime is considered _pest_ if you commit it knowing that you were doing something unlawful.

7. _____ _____ is when, without thinking, you do something that you should have known could result in somebody getting hurt—and somebody does end up hurt because of your actions.

8. _____ is when somebody entrusts you with his property or money to take care of, but you decide to use the property or money for yourself without permission from the person(s) who gave it to you.

9. Taking somebody's property through threat of force or physical violence is called _BOD_.

3

10. _Burglary_ is when a person illegally, or without proper permission, goes into a building or home with the intent to commit a crime (like stealing) once inside.

11. _____ can be defined as unlawful use of force.

12. _____ occurs when you make a person feel that you are going to immediately bring physical harm to a person.

13. The killing of a human being by another person is known as _____.

14. The homicide crime of _____ is usually considered the most serious homicide crime.

15. Picking on, and harassing, someone such that it interferes with his education or school environment is _bullying_.

16. _____ _____ is an unintentional killing of a human being by another human being. It usually occurs because of carelessness or recklessness.

17. Even if you do not carry out a crime, you can be charged with the crime of _____.

18. You can be charged with the crime of _____ if you agree to help somebody commit a crime.

19. A(n) _____ is a person who helps somebody commit a crime.

20. _____ occurs when a person of a certain age has sex with a person under a certain age and to do so is illegal.

True or False

Directions

Decide if the following statement is True or False. Circle True or False.

21. Only "bad" people can be labeled as criminals.

    True   False ✓

22. You cannot be punished for breaking the law if you had no idea that you were breaking the law.

    True ✓   False

23. It is important that you think and care about the consequences of your actions.

    True ✓   False

24. Carelessness can lead to your being charged with a serious crime.

    True ✓   False

25. You should never ever take risks in life.

    True ✓   False

26. Embezzlement involves taking someone's things using the threat of violence.

    True   False ✓

27. You cannot be accused of shoplifting unless you walk out of the store with the stolen merchandise.

    True   False ✓

28. Everybody involved in a conspiracy can be charged with whatever other crimes people involved in the conspiracy did to move the conspiracy along.

    True   False ✓

29. In order to get involved in a conspiracy, you have to verbally agree to be a part of it.

    True   False ✓

30. A charge of murder always involves serious planning and plotting to kill somebody.

    True   False ✓

31. Involuntary manslaughter is usually considered as serious as murder.

    True ✓   False

32. You can avoid being punished for committing a strict liability crime if you can prove that you really didn't intend to break the law.

    True   False ✓

33. You cannot be charged with any crimes for engaging in sexting or cyberbullying.

    True   False ✓

34. If a person made threats in anger to "blow up" his school, these would never be taken seriously by law enforcement.

    True   False ✓

35. Underage drinking is okay if you can handle it.

    True   False ✓

36. If you are around people who are using drugs but you are not, the police will leave you alone.

    True   False ✓

37. The police cannot arrest you for yelling and cursing at them, as long as you don't touch them or physically get in their personal space.

    True   False ✓

38. If someone threatens to kill you if you do not kill someone else for them, the law will not punish you if you carry out the killing.

    True   False ✓

39. You have every right to use any amount of force you want to use if somebody is attacking you.

    True ✓   False

40. You can never use force to keep somebody from taking your things.

    True   False ✓

Multiple Choice

Directions

Please circle the best answer.

41. Which of the following is a crime that always involves property?
    A. Conspiracy
    B. Embezzlement
    C. Solicitation
    D. Attempt

42. The act of asking, encouraging, hiring, or commanding somebody to commit a crime.
    A. Solicitation
    B. Battery
    C. Conspiracy
    D. Assault

43. The sending or forwarding of nude or sexually suggestive or explicit pictures to a cell phone.
    A. Solicitation
    B. Conspiracy
    C. Sexting
    D. Robbery

44. A situation where you have no choice but to hurt somebody else to keep them from hurting you.
    A. Robbery
    B. Battery
    C. Self-Defense
    D. Sexting

45. Special excuses and justifications that allow you to avoid being punished by the criminal justice system.
    A. Battery
    B. Conspiracy
    C. Law
    D. Legal Defenses

46. An intentional illegal burning of a building.
    A. Arson
    B. Graffiti
    C. Robbery
    D. Embezzlement

47. A crime that occurs when a person hurts someone else by unthinkingly doing something risky or dangerous that he or she should have known could lead to someone getting hurt.
    A. Criminal Recklessness
    B. Criminal Negligence
    C. Assault
    D. Battery

48. The person who has the job of proving in court that you committed the crime that you're being accused of.
    A. Bailiff
    B. Prosecutor
    C. Judge
    D. Public Defender

49. A crime that is punishable by up to a year in jail.
    A. Murder
    B. Arson
    C. Felony
    D. Misdemeanor

50. The legal defense used by a person who commits a crime only because he was forced to by someone who threatened to hurt him if he did not commit the crime.
    A. Duress
    B. Mistake of Fact
    C. Self-Defense
    D. Defense of Others

NAME _____ DATE _____

CHAPTER 1
Exercise

FILL IN THE BLANK

Directions
Using context clues in the passage, fill in the blanks with the correct term from the list.
You will not use all of the terms on the list.

bad	harm	order	murder	robbery	criminals	freedom
break	laws	result	punish	safe	authorities	privileges
fine	obey	prison	right	wrong	dangerous	reckless

Every society has to keep its citizens _____. It must also have rules for people

to follow so that _____ can be maintained. If there were no government rules,

also known as _____ , there would be no peace. Some people wrongly think that

only _____ people can be labeled as _____. However, the govern-

ment can and will _____ good people who _____ the law. Failure

to _____ the law can _____ in a person's loss of _____.

This could mean some time spent in jail or _____. Sometimes a person may

have to pay a _____ when she breaks the law. In other cases, a person may lose

certain _____ such as the suspension of her driver's license.

Although many laws are based on principles of right and _____ , some may

seem to be random or silly. Still, every citizen, and even non-citizens, are required to stay

within the law. There are many different crimes that the government will discipline people

for committing such as the very serious crimes of _____ and _____.

While we may not always agree with all of the laws that are enforced by the _____ ,

without them life would be very _____.

NAME _____ DATE _____

CHAPTER 1
Group Activity

GETTING TO KNOW YOU

THE NICKNAME GAME

Directions

- You will be placed into groups of three to five participants.

- Sit in a circle on the floor.

- The first person in the circle will give the group his or her full name and a nickname that best describes him or her to the group. Example: Mike Jones, "Magnificent Mike."

- The next person will tell the group their full name then a nickname that best describes him or her to the group and repeats the name of the person(s) who preceded them: Tay Brown, "Terrific Tay," Magnificent Mike, etc.

- Remember each person must give his or her name and the nickname of all the people who introduced themselves before him or her all the way back to the first person in the group.

- Repeat until each person has had an opportunity to participate.

NAME _____ DATE _____

CHAPTER 2
Group Activity #2

WE COULD BE COUSINS!

Rationale

The purpose of this interview exercise is to give participants an opportunity to learn more about each other and what you may have in common. The exercise is designed to foster inquiry and communication skills. It is also an opportunity to help participants become comfortable presenting in a public setting.

Directions

- Participants are divided into groups of two each. Each person is given an interview sheet with a list of sample questions he or she can ask their interview partner.

- Each person must interview the other. (Switch after five minutes)

- Each student will introduce his or her partner to the whole group using information gathered during the interview.

- Groups will be given about fifteen minutes to conduct both interviews and make notes.

- Feel free to use the interview form provided in your workbook.

WE COULD BE COUSINS!	
INTERVIEWEE:	**INTERVIEWER:**
DIRECTIONS: Please interview your partner and write your notes below. Use this information to introduce your partner to the group.	
Interview Questions	
Use the questions below and feel free to make up your own questions.	
Tell me about your family? How many brothers and sisters do you have? Where were you born?	

How did you get your name?	
What is your favorite food and favorite dessert?	
Who is your favorite relative?	
What is your favorite movie, video game or TV show?	
What is the funniest thing you ever saw?	
What is your favorite thing to do?	
What do you think you do best?	
YOUR QUESTION?	

CHAPTER 2
Exercise #1

TYPES OF CRIMES

Read the **Terms** that appear in the left column. Read the **Meanings** in the right column. Match the term in the left column with the appropriate meaning in the right column by writing the number of the meaning in the column titled "MATCH."

TERMS	MATCH	MEANINGS
1. Intentional		I. A person does something with less care than she should and it results in a harm that she should have known could happen.
2. Willful Blindness		II. A person knows a certain action is risky and could result in harm to someone, but chooses to do the action anyway.
3. Criminal Recklessness		III. A person knows a certain action is a crime and does the action.
4. Criminal Negligence		IV. Purposely not finding out all the facts about something so you can say you didn't know what was going on.

NAME _____ DATE _____

CHAPTER 2
Exercise #2

ACTION, RESPONSE AND JUDGMENT

Directions

Not thinking about the consequences of your actions could lead to your being charged with a serious crime. Go back and reread the scenario about Tamika on page 8 of the text. After you have finished, answer the questions in the Action, Response, and Final Judgment columns below. If you are doing this activity as part of a group exercise, discuss your responses with the group.

ACTION *Name and define the type of crime(s) Tamika committed.*	RESPONSE *What do you think about this situation?*	FINAL JUDGMENT *What might the law do? What would you do?*

NAME _____ DATE _____

CHAPTER 3
Exercise

DON'T BE PUZZLED ABOUT THE LAW

Directions

There are fifteen words or phrases from the chapter hidden in the puzzle. Can you find them? Circle each word that you find from the list below.

I	G	L	H	U	S	A	R	S	Y	A	U	B	H	N	Y	L
G	N	I	T	F	I	L	P	O	H	S	H	U	N	Y	R	G
T	I	G	O	R	L	I	N	O	I	S	S	I	M	R	E	P
H	L	Y	L	L	A	G	E	L	L	I	T	L	A	A	B	L
R	A	R	T	B	R	E	A	K	I	N	L	D	R	L	B	F
E	E	G	N	F	C	N	Y	A	T	A	K	I	N	G	O	P
A	T	E	M	B	E	Z	Z	L	E	M	E	N	T	R	R	L
T	S	M	L	T	N	H	S	E	R	B	B	G	C	U	A	O
O	E	Y	K	N	Y	M	T	B	L	H	Y	E	T	B	L	K

Theft	Stealing	Burglary	Taking	Embezzlement
Shoplifting	Force	Threat	Illegally	Robbery
Permission	Larceny	Break In	Building	

NAME _____ DATE _____

CHAPTER 4
Exercise

WORD SCRAMBLE

Directions

Unscramble the following words related to crimes involving violence from Chapter 4. After the words have been unscrambled, discuss the meaning of each unscrambled word.

1. AETRYBT   is _____ .

2. AAUSLTS   is _____ .

3. CSIIOHDEM   is _____ .

4. URDEMR   is _____ .

5. ILGNILK   is _____ .

6. IITLYLENOATNN   is _____ .

7. OPOKERV   is _____ .

8. GLNEEGNIT   is _____ .

9. PWNESOA   is _____ .

10. NTCHIOGU   is _____ .

NAME _____ DATE _____

CHAPTER 5
Exercise #1

HALFWAY CRIMES

Directions

Draw a line from the word to its correct meaning.

a. SNITCHING

b. CONSPIRACY

c. SOLICITATION

d. ATTEMPT

e. INCHOATE

1. INCOMPLETE CRIMES

2. THE "INCHOATE" CRIME OF TRYING TO COMMIT A CRIME

3. FIGHTING A CRIME BY REPORTING YOUR CO-CONSPIRATORS TO THE POLICE

4. AN AGREEMENT BETWEEN TWO OR MORE PEOPLE TO COMMIT A CRIME

5. IF YOU ASK, ENCOURAGE, HIRE, OR COMMAND SOMEBODY TO COMMIT A CRIME

NAME _____ DATE _____

CHAPTER 5
Exercise #2

GOT CRIME?

Directions

Collect newspaper or internet articles about a crime and answer the questions below.

1. What are the facts of the crime?

_____

_____

_____

2. What type of crime was committed?

_____

_____

_____

3. What were the consequences of committing the crime?

_____

_____

_____

NAME _____ DATE _____

CHAPTER 6
Exercise

SHOWING SMARTS

Directions

Read the statements below and select the decision you think is the "smartest" choice. Please circle your answer.

1. Your boyfriend asks you to send a special picture of yourself so he can have it to look at to remember you always. Do you
   A. take a picture in your underwear with your phone and send it to him via picture mail, or
   B. take a picture of your face with your best smile and send it to him?

2. Your girlfriend asks to take a picture of you with nothing on but your boxers so she can always see your hot body. Do you
   A. tell her you will let her take a picture of you in your basketball shorts and tank top because they really show off your arms and leg muscles, or
   B. take your shirt and shorts off and pose in your boxers for the photo?

3. A friend of yours forwards you a naked picture of his girlfriend to show off. Do you
   A. keep the picture in your phone and high five your friend the next time you see him, or
   B. delete the picture and tell your friend not to send anymore naked pictures of his girl to you?

4. A naked picture of a really hot guy is going around cell phones at school. A friend forwards it to you. Do you
   A. delete the picture and go about your normal school day, or
   B. send it to your best friend to make sure she gets it too?

5. Your older brother asks you to forward a picture of a classmate in her pajama shorts and brassiere that you took at a guys and girls sleepover. Do you
   A. tell him no and refuse to send the picture to anyone, or
   B. tell him no and delete the picture from your phone forever?

NAME _____ DATE _____

CHAPTER 7
Group Activity

BULLYING THE BULLY

Directions
Break into groups of two. Work with your partner to identify possible instances of bullying within your school based on what you learned in Chapter 7. Write them out below. Next, work with your partner to plan a way to stop it. Write your plan below.

GROUP NOTES

_____

_____

_____

_____

_____

_____

_____

_____

_____

NAME _____ DATE _____

CHAPTER 8
Exercise

FILL IN THE MISSING WORD

Directions

Fill in the blanks with a word that best completes the sentence. Refer back to Chapter 8 of your textbook for clues and hints about the words that should be used.

1. Starting fires can result in a charge for the crime of _____.

2. _____ of someone's property is a crime, and may even be a felony.

3. You may get locked up for _____ if you are rude and get an attitude with a police officer when she asks you questions about a crime.

4. You shouldn't make _____ _____ toward people when you get mad at them because you can end up charged with a crime for it.

5. _____ impairs brain function and is actually classified as a poison.

6. Even if you are not trying to sell _____ just having them can get a criminal charge with _____ _____.

7. Acting crazy in public may cause a police officer to arrest you for _____ _____.

8. Minor acts can sometimes result in serious _____.

9. People should never _____ and _____ because doing so can lead to horrible accidents.

10. If you hit and kill someone while drunk driving you can be charged with _____.

NAME _____ DATE _____

General Review
Exercise #1

NAME THAT CRIME

Directions

Indicate by circling your response whether the incidents below are lawful or criminal. If it is a criminal act then Name That Crime.

1. A young teen is traveling home on the school bus. After taking a sip of her soft drink, she purposely spills the soda on the seat of the bus. Is this criminal or lawful?

   Criminal   Lawful   Not Sure

   Name That Crime _____

2. A teen is trying to light a firecracker in the garage and accidentally starts a fire that burns up a car and the garage of a neighbor. Is this criminal or lawful?

   Criminal   Lawful   Not Sure

   Name That Crime _____

3. A teen takes a bag across state lines for a known drug dealer and returns with another bag. He transports the bags without knowing the contents. Is this criminal or lawful?

   Criminal   Lawful   Not Sure

   Name That Crime _____

4. A mother leaves her four-year-old daughter and baby sister home alone to go to the store to purchase bread, eggs, cereal, and milk for the infant. Is this criminal or lawful?

    Criminal   Lawful   Not Sure

    Name That Crime _____

5. A young man is angry at his math teacher for embarrassing him in class after giving an incorrect answer. The student comes to school the next day and leaves a note on the teacher's desk before class telling the teacher "You better watch your back" and "I am going to get you after school." Is this criminal or lawful?

    Criminal   Lawful   Not Sure

    Name That Crime _____

6. A guy in the neighborhood is at your house and is talking with your cousin about a plan to steal some small electronics from Best Buy. He knows a guy who works for the store who will let them in the back when the store closes. Is this criminal or lawful?

    Criminal   Lawful   Not Sure

    Name That Crime _____

NAME _____ DATE _____

General Review
Exercise #2

CRIMINAL JUSTICE QUIZ GAME

What You Will Need

1. First eight chapters of *When the Cops Come Knockin'* text/workbook. You will be assigned chapters as follows:

   • Team A – Chapters 1, 2, 3, and 4

   • Team B – Chapters 5, 6, 7, and 8

2. Paper and pencil for each student

3. A person to serve as a recorder for each team

4. A person to serve as the spokesperson for each team

Directions

Day One: The Setup

• Divide into Teams A and B. Each team will be assigned four chapters from the first eight chapters in the text/workbook. Each team member is to silently read the chapters to himself/herself. Each team member will highlight any information in the chapters that could be used in the upcoming game. Each person is to write three possible questions developed from the text he or she read and the answers to those questions.

• When everyone is finished reading, Team A will come together on one side of the room. Team B will come together on the other side of the room. Each team is to settle on fifteen questions from all of the submitted questions to use in the game. Each team must also assign a point value for each question based on the question's degree of difficulty. The point value must be 2, 4, or 6. There must be an equal number of easy to difficult questions. In other words, five must be assigned a value of 2, five must be assigned a value of 4, and five must be assigned a value of 6. Each question and answer sheet should have the assigned team's name on it so that the facilitator will know which team wrote the question.

- Each team should choose a person to act as a recorder who will use a sheet of paper to draft the question and answer sheet and to record each team participant's name and hand it to the facilitator. Lastly, the recorder will keep track of points that his/her team amasses.

Day Two: The Game

- You are to get into your team and choose a spokesperson. The facilitator will choose a team to begin and allow the starting team an opportunity to answer a question. When it is your team's turn to answer a question, you will have to decide as a team which point value question you would like (2, 4, or 6). The team has only fifteen seconds to come up with a point value. Once the team has chosen a point value, the spokesperson then tells the facilitator, "We choose a 2 (or 4 or 6) point question." Remember, the higher the point value, the more difficult the question.

- The facilitator will then read the question. Your team will have twenty seconds to come up with the answer to the question—only the spokesperson can announce your answer to the facilitator.

- If the question is answered correctly, your team will be awarded the points. If the answer is incorrect, your team will not receive points.

- Each team take turns selecting questions until the game is completed. The team with the highest point total wins.

NAME _____ DATE _____

CHAPTER 9
Exercise #1

AGREE OR DISAGREE

Directions

Read each statement and think about whether you agree or disagree. Circle either Agree or Disagree. If you are not sure circle the **"?."** Discuss your answers with the group.

1. If you mistakenly shoot the wrong person while intending to unjustifiably shoot someone, the law will excuse you.   Agree   **"?"**   Disagree

2. You are expected to know every law.   Agree   **"?"**   Disagree

3. The law may excuse you if you steal from a local clothing store because someone threatened to hurt you if you didn't help them shoplift.   Agree   **"?"**   Disagree

Exercise #2

DRAWING THE LINE

Directions

Draw a line from the word to the statement you think matches best.

1. Legal Defenses

2. Mistake of Fact

3. Duress

A. being forced to commit a crime, usually under threat of violence

B. excuses and justifications for doing something that is usually considered unlawful

C. doing something illegal because you perceived something incorrectly, but had no intention of doing anything illegal

NAME _____ DATE _____

CHAPTER 9
Exercise #3

BUT OFFICER, IT WAS SELF-DEFENSE!

Directions

The use of self-defense has special rules. When can you use self-defense? Read the following statements and circle "Yes" or "No" as to whether self-defense can or cannot be used. If you are not sure, circle Maybe.

1. You are allowed to immediately attack a bully who says he is going to beat you up two days from today.

    Yes   No   Maybe

2. A person can threaten to use a gun in self-defense if a robber pulls a knife on him in an alley.

    Yes   No   Maybe

3. Deadly force can always be used to protect personal property.

    Yes   No   Maybe

4. If a person jumps at you unprovoked with a roundhouse kick, is it considered an immediate and unlawful threat of violence?

    Yes   No   Maybe

5. You can use self-defense when someone makes jokes about you in front of a crowd of your friends.

    Yes   No   Maybe

6. A homeowner can shoot a burglar when the burglar is clearly leaving the house.

    Yes   No   Maybe

7. Instead of going to the police, you should take it upon yourself to use force to get back property stolen from you last week.

    Yes   No   Maybe

NAME _____ DATE _____

CHAPTER 9
Exercise #4

PROSECUTOR VS. DEFENSE ATTORNEY

Directions

You are to choose a partner and select who will be the prosecutor and who will be the defense attorney. Each partner should help the other brainstorm two situations in which someone can use self-defense as an excuse and two situations in which someone cannot use self-defense as an excuse.

The prosecutor will present two situations in which self-defense cannot be used as an excuse.

_____

_____

_____

_____

The defense attorney will present two situations in which self-defense can be used as an excuse.

_____

_____

_____

_____

NAME _____ DATE _____

CHAPTER 10
Exercise

DO THE RIGHT THING

Directions

Circle the letter of the answer that best represents the "Right Thing" to do in each situation.

1. **A homeless man gets hit by a car in front of the school. You should:**

    A. Run after the driver and throw rocks.

    B. Use your cell phone to call for help and don't cause further harm to the victim unless you are qualified to give first aid.

    C. Leave the victim because it is not your problem.

2. **A group of boys that you know are throwing bricks off the highway overpass but you are not. If a stranger in a car below is hit does the law require you to go help?**

    A. Yes

    B. No

3. **A four-year-old boy is seen drowning in a swimming pool and you are a lifeguard. You should:**

    A. Call the other lifeguard on duty.

    B. Pull the victim out of the water and administer CPR as you learned in your lifeguard training class.

    C. Take your lunch break.

4. **Your boss sees a pot on the stove in the lunchroom has caught fire and flames are everywhere. He should:**

    A. Pull the fire alarm and run out of the building without making sure other employees are safe.

    B. Skip pulling the fire alarm and run down the stairs and out of the building without saying anything to anyone.

    C. Pull the fire alarm and try to evacuate all employees if he can safely do so.

NAME _____ DATE _____

PART I: CRIMES AND CRIMINAL OFFENSES
POST-TEST
Fill in the Blank

Directions

Please fill in the blanks with the correct answer.

1. A _____ is the classification given a person after committing a crime.

2. _____ are government rules to keep order and protect people.

3. _____ is no excuse for breaking the law.

4. _____ is the taking of somebody else's property with the intent to keep it.

5. _____ _____ occurs when you ignore clues and facts that would alert you that you are doing, or are about to do, something unlawful.

6. A crime is considered _____ if you commit it knowing that you were doing something unlawful.

7. _____ _____ is when, without thinking, you do something that you should have known could result in somebody getting hurt—and somebody does end up hurt because of your actions.

8. _____ is when somebody entrusts you with his property or money to take care of, but you decide to use the property or money for yourself without permission from the person(s) who gave it to you.

9. Taking somebody's property through threat of force or physical violence is called _____.

10. _____ is when a person illegally, or without proper permission, goes into a building or home with the intent to commit a crime (like stealing) once inside.

11. _____ can be defined as unlawful use of force.

12. _____ occurs when you make a person feel that you are going to immediately bring physical harm to a person.

13. The killing of a human being by another person is known as _____.

14. The homicide crime of _____ is usually considered the most serious homicide crime.

15. Picking on, and harassing, someone such that it interferes with his education or school environment is _____.

16. _____ _____ is an unintentional killing of a human being by another human being. It usually occurs because of carelessness or recklessness.

17. Even if you do not carry out a crime, you can be charged with the crime of _____.

18. You can be charged with the crime of _____ if you agree to help somebody commit a crime.

19. A(n) _____ is a person who helps somebody commit a crime.

20. _____ _____ occurs when a person of a certain age has sex with a person under a certain age and to do so is illegal.

True or False

Directions

Decide if the following statement is True or False. Circle True or False.

21. Only "bad" people can be labeled as criminals.

    True   False

22. You cannot be punished for breaking the law if you had no idea that you were breaking the law.

    True   False

23. It is important that you think and care about the consequences of your actions.

    True   False

24. Carelessness can lead to your being charged with a serious crime.

    True   False

25. You should never ever take risks in life.

    True   False

26. Embezzlement involves taking someone's things using the threat of violence.

    True   False

27. You cannot be accused of shoplifting unless you walk out of the store with the stolen merchandise.

    True   False

28. Everybody involved in a conspiracy can be charged with whatever other crimes people involved in the conspiracy did to move the conspiracy along.

    True   False

29. In order to get involved in a conspiracy, you have to verbally agree to be a part of it.

    True   False

30. A charge of murder always involves serious planning and plotting to kill somebody.

    True   False

31. Involuntary manslaughter is usually considered as serious as murder.

    True   False

32. You can avoid being punished for committing a strict liability crime if you can prove that you really didn't intend to break the law.

    True   False

33. You cannot be charged with any crimes for engaging in sexting or cyberbullying.

    True   False

34. If a person made threats in anger to "blow up" his school, these would never be taken seriously by law enforcement.

    True   False

35. Underage drinking is okay if you can handle it.

    True   False

36. If you are around people who are using drugs but you are not, the police will leave you alone.

    True   False

37. The police cannot arrest you for yelling and cursing at them, as long as you don't touch them or physically get in their personal space.

    True   False

38. If someone threatens to kill you if you do not kill someone else for them, the law will not punish you if you carry out the killing.

    True   False

39. You have every right to use any amount of force you want to use if somebody is attacking you.

    True   False

40. You can never use force to keep somebody from taking your things.

    True   False

Multiple Choice

Directions

Please circle the best answer.

41. Which of the following is a crime that always involves property?

    A. Conspiracy

    B. Embezzlement

    C. Solicitation

    D. Attempt

42. The act of asking, encouraging, hiring, or commanding somebody to commit a crime.

    A. Solicitation

    B. Battery

    C. Conspiracy

    D. Assault

43. The sending or forwarding of nude or sexually suggestive or explicit pictures to a cell phone.

    A. Solicitation

    B. Conspiracy

    C. Sexting

    D. Robbery

44. A situation where you have no choice but to hurt somebody else to keep them from hurting you.

    A. Robbery

    B. Battery

    C. Self-Defense

    D. Sexting

45. Special excuses and justifications that allow you to avoid being punished by the criminal justice system.

    A. Battery

    B. Conspiracy

    C. Law

    D. Legal Defenses

46. An intentional illegal burning of a building.

    A. Arson

    B. Graffiti

    C. Robbery

    D. Embezzlement

47. A crime that occurs when a person hurts someone else by unthinkingly doing something risky or dangerous that he or she should have known could lead to someone getting hurt.

    A. Criminal Recklessness

    B. Criminal Negligence

    C. Assault

    D. Battery

48. The person who has the job of proving in court that you committed the crime that you're being accused of.

    A. Bailiff

    B. Prosecutor

    C. Judge

    D. Public Defender

49. A crime that is punishable by up to a year in jail.

    A. Murder

    B. Arson

    C. Felony

    D. Misdemeanor

50. The legal defense used by a person who commits a crime only because he was forced to by someone who threatened to hurt him if he did not commit the crime.

    A. Duress

    B. Mistake of Fact

    C. Self-Defense

    D. Defense of Others

PART II

YOUR RIGHTS WHEN DEALING WITH THE POLICE

PART II: YOUR RIGHTS WHEN DEALING WITH THE POLICE

PRE-TEST

Fill in the Blank

Directions

Please fill in the blanks with the correct answer.

1. A _____ is basically a permission slip signed by a judge saying it is okay to invade your privacy and conduct a search of your property.

2. _____ _____ is the set of "reasons" the police have to give to the judge in order to get a warrant.

3. A _____ occurs when the police take your possessions.

4. An _____ is when the police do not allow you to leave when you want.

5. Being singled out by a biased cop due to probable cause is _____.

6. _____ _____ is when the police need only a very tiny reason to believe something is going down.

7. The police have to obey _____ for searches and seizures.

8. Your _____ is considered the "danger zone" because the police are allowed to search it without following as many procedures as they would to search your home.

9. The _____ sets limits on the powers of law enforcement and the government in general.

10. You have an expectation of _____ in certain places and situations. The police must respect that expectation.

True or False

Directions

Decide if the following statement is True or False. Circle True or False.

11. The police are allowed to enter your home for any reason they want to.

    True   False

12. Reasonable suspicion and probable cause are the same thing.

    True   False

13. If the police come to your house without a warrant, but want to come in, you can refuse to consent to their entering your home.

    True   False

14. Search warrants that are not signed by a judge or magistrate can still be used to enter your home.

    True   False

15. You are only under arrest when the police tell you that you are under arrest.

    True   False

16. If the police stop you on the street, you should answer any questions that they ask you.

    True   False

17. If you didn't do anything wrong, you have no reason to refuse if the police ask to search your property.

    True   False

18. When cops want to search your car, they have to follow the exact same rules that apply to them searching your home.

    True   False

19. The best way to find out if you're under arrest is to ask.

    True   False

20. Depending on the neighborhood you're in, the police are allowed to chase you, stop you and frisk you if you start running when you see them approaching.

    True   False

Multiple Choice

Directions

Please circle the correct answer.

21. If you are stopped by the police in a car, you should:
    A. be polite and talk as calmly as you can
    B. get out and run
    C. take a call on your cell phone
    D. not let down your window

22. If the police come knocking at your door with a search warrant, you should:
    A. not open the door
    B. get out and run
    C. open the door and read the warrant to make sure it's legitimate
    D. yell at the police and tell them to go away

23. A warrant is not legitimate if:
    A. it is not signed by a judge
    B. the address is wrong
    C. it was not approved in the last two weeks
    D. all of the above

24. If a cop walks up to you on the street and asks to have a look at your personal items, such as a bag, purse, or backpack, you should:
    A. run away from the cop
    B. not give them permission
    C. yell at the cop to get away
    D. ignore the cop

25. If the police trash your house during a search, you should:
    A. physically attack them for trashing your house
    B. demand that the police clean your house
    C. yell and curse at the police
    D. take pictures and give them to your attorney

26. When you are under arrest by the police, you should:
    A. fight back
    B. continue to talk to the police
    C. remain silent
    D. try to run away

27. If the police come to your door without a warrant, you should:
    A. step outside and talk to them
    B. ignore them
    C. yell and threaten them
    D. open the door slightly and talk to them through that slightly opened door

28. When throwing a party, you should:
    A. keep all of your doors shut
    B. not invite anyone who has a history of drug use
    C. keep your music at a reasonable level
    D. all of the above

29. To avoid drawing police attention to yourself when driving, you should:

    A. have the darkest tint legally allowable on your windows

    B. blast your music as loud as possible

    C. be careful about modifying or "tricking" your car out

    D. throw trash onto the highway

30. If you are arrested, you should:

    A. start explaining to them why you're innocent

    B. try to walk or run away

    C. exercise your right to remain silent

    D. all of the above

NAME _____ DATE _____

CHAPTER 11
Exercise #1

A LITTLE HISTORY

Directions

Please fill in the blanks with the appropriate answer.

1. The ill treatment of people by King _____ of _____ caused a revolution and the new country to adopt the Constitution.

2. _____ keeps the police from mistreating people.

3. The _____, _____, and _____ Amendments to the Constitution give you special rights and prevent abuse by the police.

4. If you can show the police _____ your rights you may be able to avoid conviction.

5. Being stopped by the _____ can be a very _____ situation.

BEEN STOPPED?

Exercise #2

Discussion Question: Have you or someone else you know ever been stopped by the police? Please write down what happened.

_____

_____

_____

_____

NAME _____ DATE _____

CHAPTER 12
Exercise #1

DON'T BE PUZZLED ABOUT THE LAW

Directions

There are ten words from the chapter hidden in the puzzle. Can you find them? Circle each word that you find from the list below.

P	D	F	H	C	B	E	Y	M	G	N	J	P
R	R	C	D	Q	V	C	E	H	U	M	K	L
I	S	O	C	X	W	N	R	S	D	V	N	P
V	C	N	B	T	O	R	H	E	L	P	M	P
A	Y	D	I	A	I	A	U	T	O	B	O	V
C	B	U	M	G	B	W	H	I	T	S	E	F
Y	W	C	H	E	G	L	Z	F	S	L	R	H
P	C	T	W	C	V	H	E	E	J	Q	U	Q
J	S	E	A	R	C	H	S	C	W	Z	Z	M
F	M	I	L	E	S	S	N	F	A	R	I	E
D	B	F	S	P	I	A	A	A	R	U	E	X
Q	E	G	C	O	B	G	T	C	R	G	S	J
Z	C	M	N	T	S	E	C	E	A	H	P	E
X	A	S	B	M	K	N	H	B	N	T	A	H
J	S	G	R	Q	P	C	U	Q	T	O	W	T
W	E	D	F	B	M	U	P	I	P	E	V	U

Case	Warrant	Snatch Up	Conduct
Search	Seizure	Probable Cause	Possessions
Rights	Privacy		

NAME _____ DATE _____

CHAPTER 12
Exercise #2

U BE THE JUDGE

Directions

First, determine if you agree or disagree with the statements before and put an "X" in the box with your answer.

Next, divide up into small groups of four. Each group of four must break up into two smaller groups of two and designate one small group "Team A" and the other "Team B." Team A is to present reasons why the class should agree with the statement. Team B will present reasons why the class should disagree with the statement. Participants are to write down key points and issues. Disband the teams and have an entire class discussion of the key points and issues that participants wrote down.

STATEMENTS	AGREE	DISAGREE
1. If the police have a hunch, they have the right to search anyone in your home without permission.		
2. You should expect privacy protection when you are in school or at work.		
3. Police officers should have no restrictions on fighting crime.		
4. If most of the information on a search warrant is correct, the police should be able to use it to search your home or things.		

NAME _____ DATE _____

CHAPTER 13
Exercise

FILL IN THE BLANK

Directions

Using context clues in the passage, fill in the blanks with the correct term from the list. You will not use all of the terms on the list.

arrest	apartment	drugs	enter	force	attorney	refuse
judge	responsibility	hurt	lock	guests	legitimate	search
party	permission	old	slang	knock	warrant	

If the police _____ at your door, you should be prepared. Sometimes the police will want to come in to your home to conduct a _____ but will not have a _____. A valid warrant must be signed by a _____ or magistrate and should be dated fairly recently. It should also have the correct address. If you live in an _____, the warrant should have the correct building and unit number. A warrant that is missing these things is not _____, meaning it is not valid, and the police are not supposed to _____ your home. However, they may get around having to obtain a warrant by merely asking you for _____ to come in. Of course, you can _____ to consent to their entering, and it is usually a good idea to do so. If the police do not have a warrant and you do not consent to their entering your home, they are not allowed in unless someone is in danger or they are chasing a suspect who runs into the home. After your refusal, they are not supposed to _____ you to let them in. If the police go into your home after you've told them no, you should never try to physically stop them. Instead, be sure to tell your _____ that they entered despite your refusal.

NAME _____ DATE _____

CHAPTER 13
Group Activity

"BUZZWORDS"

Directions

Each player is given several index cards. You are to write a word related to crime, criminal law or the justice system at the top of the card and then draw a line under the word. Below the main word participants must also write five words that the person giving the clues is banned from saying. For instance, if the word is "jail" the banned words might be "bars," "bail," "sheriff," "lock," or "cell."

Each participant should make five to six cards. All of the cards should be put into a hat or box to be shuffled.

You will be divided into two teams. A clue-giver of the first team should be chosen to go first. The clue-giver will pick a card and attempt to get her team to guess the word. But, the clue-giver must not use any of the banned words. Gestures are not permitted.

Someone from the opposing team monitors the clue-giver by looking over the clue-giver's shoulder to make sure that the clue giver does not mistakenly say the banned word. If the clue-giver slips up and says the banned word, the monitor gets to "buzz" her (either with a supplied buzzer, bell or just verbally). A buzz means that the clue-giver must stop and the turn then goes to the opposing team. Each team is given one minute to guess as many words as they can. Time should be kept by a member of the opposing team.

Scoring is one point for each word guessed correctly.

NAME _____ DATE _____

CHAPTER 14
Exercise

MAY I SEE YOUR LICENSE?

Directions

Circle either Agree or Disagree. If you are not sure circle the **"?."**

1. Cops do not have to obtain a warrant to search your car.

     Agree   **"?"**   Disagree

2. You should always allow an officer to search your car if they ask nicely.

     Agree   **"?"**   Disagree

3. The law does not require you to carry your license, insurance, and registration while driving.

     Agree   **"?"**   Disagree

4. If you are arrested by the cops, you should refuse to answer questions until you speak with an attorney.

     Agree   **"?"**   Disagree

Listing

5. List five things you should not do if your car is pulled over by the cops.

     A. _____

     B. _____

     C. _____

     D. _____

     E. _____

NAME _____ DATE _____

CHAPTER 15
Exercise

ABC'S OF ARREST

Directions

Write the letter of the best choice.

1. _____ You are under arrest when
   A. the cops start questioning you
   B. you are not free to leave the police
   C. the cops take you down to the station
   D. all of the above

2. _____ The cops are required to read you your rights whenever they arrest you
   A. True
   B. False

3. _____ If you are arrested you should exercise your right to
   A. ask the police to call your mom
   B. remain silent and request to speak to an attorney
   C. just walk away
   D. all of the above

4. _____ Rules of arrest include
   A. Cops must have probable cause
   B. Cops cannot arrest you in a public place
   C. A and B
   D. None of the above

NAME _____ DATE _____

CHAPTER 16
Group Activity

YOUR TURN

Directions

You will write and perform a rap song or poem that educates about crime, criminal law or the criminal justice system.

You are not limited to only the subjects and topics covered in *When the Cops Come Knockin.'* You are encouraged to rap or write a poem about any topic you wish to rap about as long as it educates about crime, criminal law or the criminal justice system. For instance, you might write lyrics about how the prisons seem to be mostly filled by the poor and/or minorities.

One very important rule is that absolutely no cursing is allowed!

NAME _____ DATE _____

PART II: YOUR RIGHTS WHEN DEALING WITH THE POLICE

POST-TEST
Fill in the Blank

Directions

Please fill in the blanks with the correct answer.

1. A _____ is basically a permission slip signed by a judge saying it is okay to invade your privacy and conduct a search of your property.

2. _____ _____ is the set of "reasons" the police have to give to the judge in order to get a warrant.

3. A _____ occurs when the police take your possessions.

4. An _____ is when the police do not allow you to leave when you want.

5. Being singled out by a biased cop due to probable cause is _____.

6. _____ _____ is when the police need only a very tiny reason to believe something is going down.

7. The police have to obey _____ for searches and seizures.

8. Your _____ is considered the "danger zone" because the police are allowed to search it without following as many procedures as they would to search your home.

9. The _____ sets limits on the powers of law enforcement and the government in general.

10. You have an expectation of _____ in certain places and situations. The police must respect that expectation.

True or False

Directions

Decide if the following statement is True or False. Circle True or False.

11. The police are allowed to enter your home for any reason they want to.

    True   False

12. Reasonable suspicion and probable cause are the same thing.

    True   False

13. If the police come to your house without a warrant, but want to come in, you can refuse to consent to their entering your home.

    True   False

14. Search warrants that are not signed by a judge or magistrate can still be used to enter your home.

    True   False

15. You are only under arrest when the police tell you that you are under arrest.

    True   False

16. If the police stop you on the street, you should answer any questions that they ask you.

    True   False

17. If you didn't do anything wrong, you have no reason to refuse if the police ask to search your property.

    True   False

18. When cops want to search your car, they have to follow the exact same rules that apply to them searching your home.

    True   False

19. The best way to find out if you're under arrest is to ask.

    True   False

20. Depending on the neighborhood you're in, the police are allowed to chase you, stop you and frisk you if you start running when you see them approaching.

    True   False

Multiple Choice

Directions

Please circle the correct answer.

21. If you are stopped by the police in a car, you should:
    A. be polite and talk as calmly as you can
    B. get out and run
    C. take a call on your cell phone
    D. not let down your window

22. If the police come knocking at your door with a search warrant, you should:
    A. not open the door
    B. get out and run
    C. open the door and read the warrant to make sure it's legitimate
    D. yell at the police and tell them to go away

23. A warrant is not legitimate if:
    A. it is not signed by a judge
    B. the address is wrong
    C. it was not approved in the last two weeks
    D. all of the above

24. If a cop walks up to you on the street and asks to have a look at your personal items, such as a bag, purse, or backpack, you should:
    A. run away from the cop
    B. not give him permission
    C. yell at the cop to get away
    D. ignore the cop

25. If the police trash your house during a search, you should:
    A. physically attack them for trashing your house
    B. demand that the police clean your house
    C. yell and curse at the police
    D. take pictures and give them to your attorney

26. When you are under arrest by the police, you should:
    A. fight back
    B. continue to talk to the police
    C. remain silent
    D. try to run away

27. If the police come to your door without a warrant, you should:
    A. step outside and talk to them
    B. ignore them
    C. yell and threaten them
    D. open the door slightly and talk to them through that slightly opened door

28. When throwing a party, you should:
    A. keep all of your doors shut
    B. not invite anyone who has a history of drug use
    C. keep your music at a reasonable level
    D. all of the above

29. To avoid drawing police attention to yourself when driving, you should:

    A. have the darkest tint legally allowable on your windows

    B. blast your music as loud as possible

    C. be careful about modifying or "tricking" your car out

    D. throw trash onto the highway

30. If you are arrested, you should:

    A. start explaining to them why you're innocent

    B. try to walk or run away

    C. exercise your right to remain silent

    D. all of the above